ENGINEERED BY NATURE

GRAND CANYON

BY MARTHA LONDON

CONTENT CONSULTANT
KARL KARLSTROM, PHD
DISTINGUISHED PROFESSOR
DEPARTMENT OF EARTH AND PLANETARY SCIENCES
UNIVERSITY OF NEW MEXICO

Kids Core
An Imprint of Abdo Publishing
abdobooks.com

abdobooks.com

Published by Abdo Publishing, a division of ABDO, PO Box 398166, Minneapolis, Minnesota 55439. Copyright © 2021 by Abdo Consulting Group, Inc. International copyrights reserved in all countries. No part of this book may be reproduced in any form without written permission from the publisher. Kids Core™ is a trademark and logo of Abdo Publishing.

Printed in the United States of America, North Mankato, Minnesota
022020
092020

Cover Photo: Sean Pavone/Shutterstock Images
Interior Photos: Anton Foltin/Shutterstock Images, 4–5; Ilex Image/iStockphoto, 6; JSC/NASA, 7; Kristen M. Caldon/National Park Service, 8; Craig Zerbe/iStockphoto, 9; Frank van den Bergh/iStockphoto, 10; Ronald Karpilo/Alamy, 12; Paige Falk/iStockphoto, 14–15; Red Line Editorial, 17, 28–29; Elena Arrigo/Shutterstock Images, 18; Erin Whittaker/National Park Service, 20–21; Library of Congress, 23; iStockphoto, 24; Maridav/Shutterstock Images, 26; Julien Hautcoeur/Shutterstock Images, 28

Editor: Marie Pearson
Series Designer: Megan Ellis

Library of Congress Control Number: 2019954239

Publisher's Cataloging-in-Publication Data

Names: London, Martha, author.
Title: Grand Canyon / by Martha London
Description: Minneapolis, Minnesota : Abdo Publishing, 2021 | Series: Engineered by nature | Includes online resources and index.
Identifiers: ISBN 9781532192869 (lib. bdg.) | ISBN 9781098210762 (ebook)
Subjects: LCSH: Grand Canyon (Ariz.)--Juvenile literature. | Natural monuments--Juvenile literature. | Canyons--Juvenile literature. | National parks and reserves--Juvenile literature. | Landforms--Juvenile literature.
Classification: DDC 910.202--dc23

CONTENTS

CHAPTER 1
Standing on the Edge 4

CHAPTER 2
Carved by Water 14

CHAPTER 3
Protecting the Canyon 20

Map 28
Glossary 30
Online Resources 31
Learn More 31
Index 32
About the Author 32

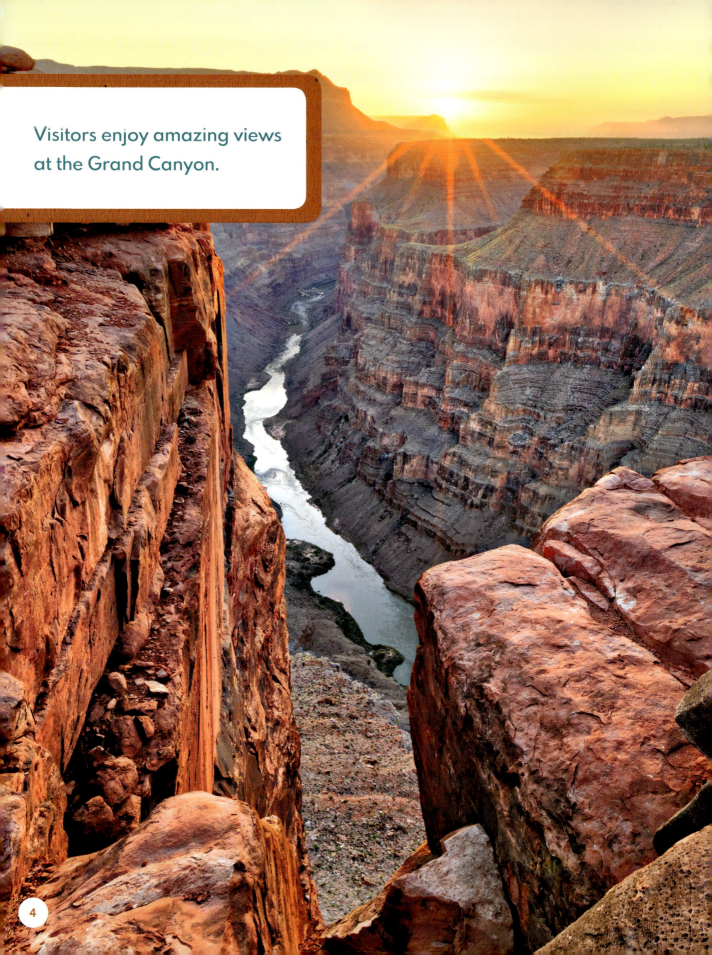

Visitors enjoy amazing views at the Grand Canyon.

CHAPTER 1

STANDING ON THE EDGE

Visitors look out over the Grand Canyon. Layers of rock stripe the canyon walls. The blue sky is bright against the orange and red rock. Visitors take pictures. They are standing at the edge of the canyon.

5

Plants grow along the riverbanks.

From where the visitors are standing, the bottom of the canyon is very deep below. A river flows at the bottom, making its way through

Satellites can photograph the Grand Canyon from space.

the canyon. This is just one of many amazing views to take in.

Layers and Layers

The Grand Canyon is massive. It is about 1 mile (1.6 km) deep. The canyon is 277 miles (446 km) long. At its widest, it is 18 miles (29 km) across. The canyon is so big that people can see it from space.

Some layers formed while the area was dry. Others formed in wet conditions.

The rocks seen in the canyon are very old. Mud, sand, and other materials hardened into rock. Basement rocks, near the canyon's bottom, formed nearly 2 billion years ago. Over time, more layers of rock built up. Each layer above the basement is a different color. That is because the rocks are made of different materials. **Minerals** and the remains of plants and animals give the layers their colors.

Rock layers at the Grand Canyon have many different colors.

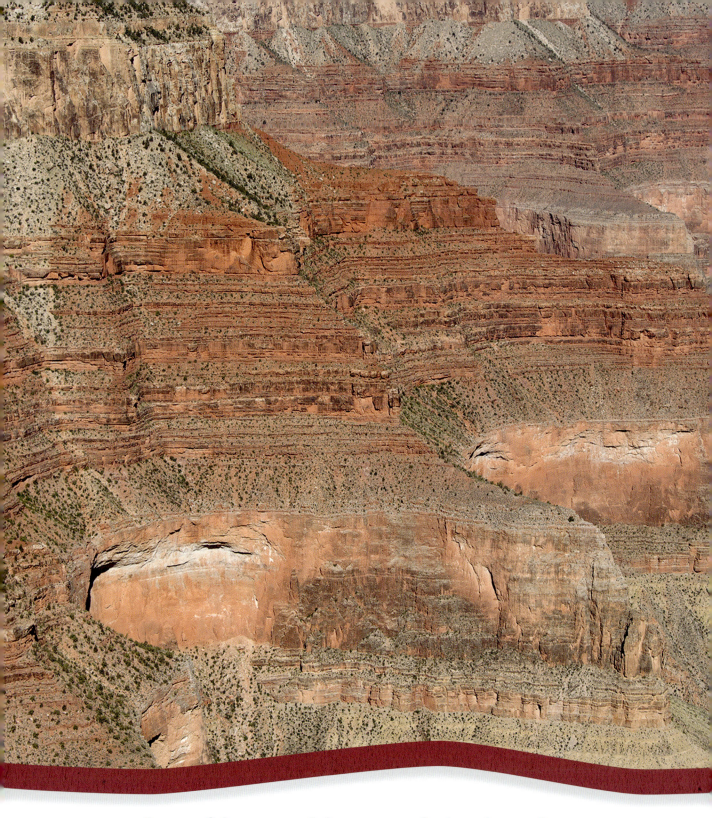

Some of the canyon's layers are thicker than others.

Each layer is from a different period of Earth's history. The layers formed in different conditions. Sometimes the area was dry. Other times rivers and shallow oceans covered this area. The layers are different thicknesses. Some layers are hundreds of feet thick.

American Indians

There are many American Indian tribes that live in and near the Grand Canyon. The Hopi believe they were created in the Grand Canyon. They call the canyon *Ongtupqa*, meaning "Salt Canyon." The Southern Paiute American Indians call the canyon *Kaibab*. The name means "Mountain Lying Down."

Scientists study the canyon's rocks to learn about its history.

There are even layers that do not exist anymore. Scientists know there should be more layers. They can test for the age of the rock in the canyon. Sometimes two layers next to each other formed millions of years apart. Wind or water swept the missing layers away soon after forming. Scientists study the layers. The layers help scientists understand Earth's early history.

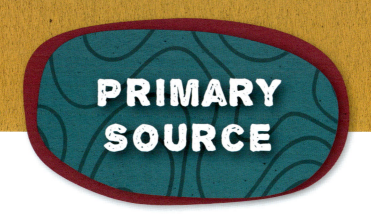

Writer Bill Bryson explained one amazing part about visiting the Grand Canyon:

> The thing that gets you—that gets everyone—is the silence. The Grand Canyon just swallows sound. The sense of space and emptiness is overwhelming.

Source: Bill Bryson. *The Lost Continent.* Harper & Row, 1989, p. 237. *Google Books.* Accessed 2 Oct. 2019.

Comparing Texts

Think about the quote. Does it support the information in this chapter? Or does it give a different perspective? Explain how in a few sentences.

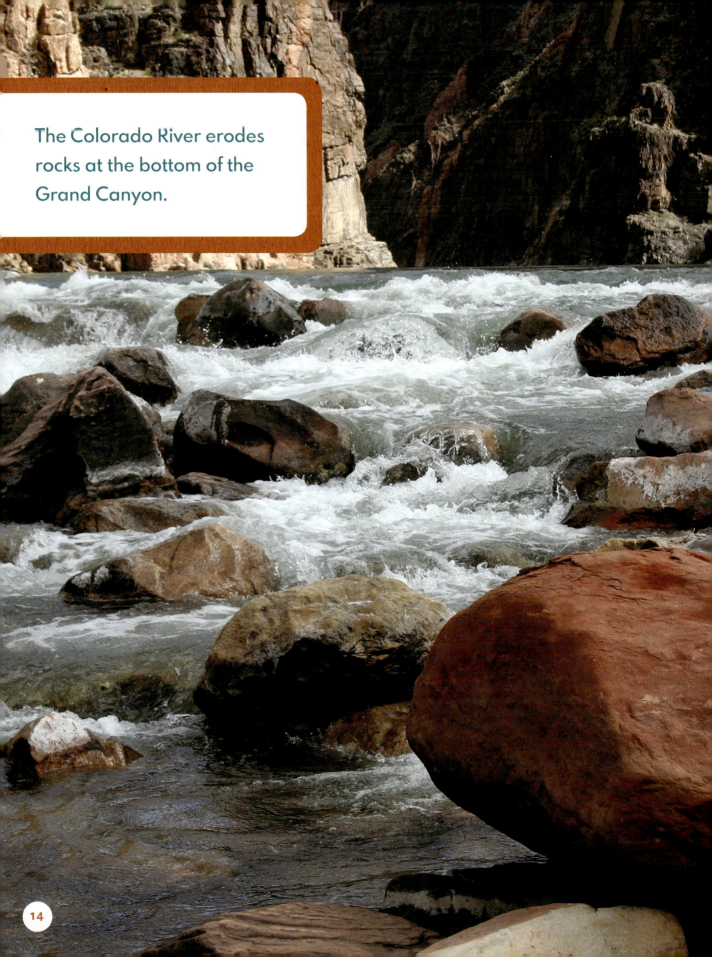

The Colorado River erodes rocks at the bottom of the Grand Canyon.

CHAPTER **2**

CARVED BY WATER

Eventually, streams and rivers began **eroding** the layers of rock. The water broke off pieces of rock and carried them away. About 70 million years ago, the ground shifted. The area rose above sea level. The area has been changing ever since then.

The Grand Canyon that people recognize today began forming approximately 6 million years ago. The Colorado River and smaller streams started carving the canyon. Landslides also widened the canyon. The river carried rocks, sand, and mud downstream to the ocean. Over time, the canyon got deeper and wider.

Each layer wears away differently. Hard rock erodes slowly. These layers form cliffs with

The Colorado River

The Colorado River carved much of the Grand Canyon. The river also provides water to many people. The river is 1,450 miles (2,330 km) long. It starts in northern Colorado and ends in Mexico. The river provides drinking water to 35 million people.

Layers of the Grand Canyon

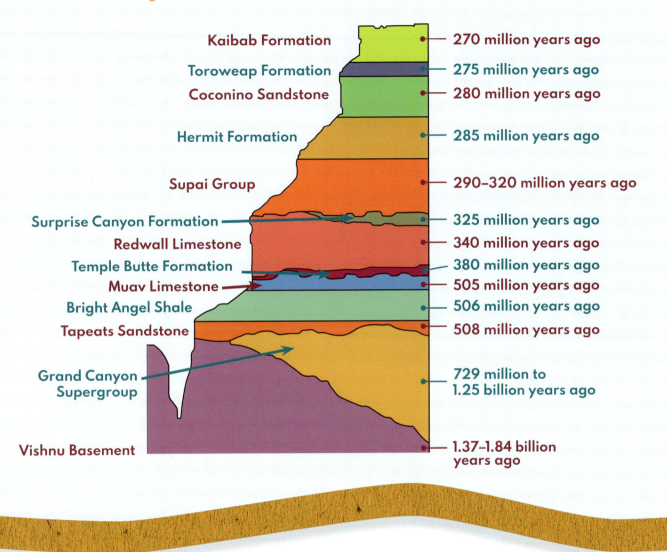

The Grand Canyon's layers tell the story of how Earth formed. The oldest rock is almost 2 billion years old.

steep sides. Soft rock erodes faster. These layers form gentle slopes.

Tourists enjoy the scenery as they raft down the Colorado River.

Still Changing

The Grand Canyon is always changing. Wind and rain are still eroding rock. The Colorado River continues to cut into the canyon. Floods cause more erosion. Rushing water pulls loose rock from the canyon. Visitors can go **rafting**. They see the canyon from the river.

At the same time, the western United States is rising very slowly. Rivers in the region used to flow in the opposite direction. However, forces deep beneath Earth's surface have pushed the land up. As the land rises, the rivers' paths have changed. They flow against different rocks. Erosion is still shaping the canyon. It is getting a little deeper each year.

Further Evidence

Look at the website below. Does it give any new evidence to support Chapter Two?

The Grand Canyon: How It Formed

abdocorelibrary.com/engineered-grand-canyon

A member of the Havasupai tribe participates in the dedication of the updated Bright Angel Trailhead in 2013.

CHAPTER 3

PROTECTING THE CANYON

People have lived in the area around the Grand Canyon for more than 13,000 years. Many of these people were farmers. Some were hunters. Today the Hopi, Navajo, Paiute, Havasupai, Hualapai, and other American Indians still live there.

European explorers first saw the canyon in 1540. In the mid-1850s, some white Americans saw the canyon. They did not see its value. They thought the canyon was worthless. But this opinion did not last long.

Theodore Roosevelt visited the Grand Canyon in 1903. He was in **awe** of its size and beauty. When he became president, Roosevelt wanted to protect the canyon. He made the Grand Canyon a national **monument** in 1908.

In 1919 President Woodrow Wilson made the Grand Canyon a national park. Many people today travel from around the world to see the canyon. The area is protected from **development**. The purpose is to preserve the park for people to enjoy into the future.

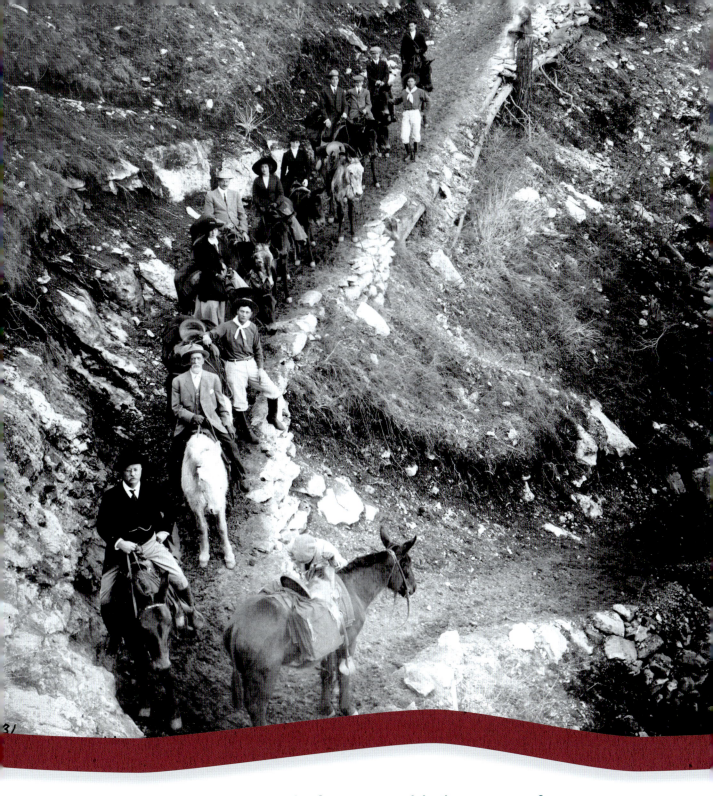

Theodore Roosevelt, *foreground*, led a group of people into the Grand Canyon in 1911.

People from all over the world enjoy Grand Canyon National Park.

24

Keeping the Canyon Clean

Today, park rangers protect the canyon. They educate visitors. Everyone has a part to play in making sure the canyon is safe for people to see for years to come. To do that, visitors must leave nothing behind. They should not throw trash on the ground. Trash can harm wildlife. It also makes the park less enjoyable for others.

Visitors

People come from all over the world to see the Grand Canyon. Fourteen percent of visitors are from a nation outside the United States. Nearly 6.4 million people visited Grand Canyon National Park in 2018.

Visitors enjoy taking beautiful photographs at the Grand Canyon.

Visitors should not leave marked trails. Leaving a trail is dangerous. People can easily get lost. And leaving a trail is also harmful to the environment. Foot traffic speeds up erosion. Some areas are more fragile than others.

The Grand Canyon is for every person to enjoy. People are not allowed to take rocks from the canyon. People should take pictures instead. When people work together to keep the canyon healthy, they can enjoy this natural wonder long into the future.

Explore Online

Visit the website below. Does it give any new information about why national parks are important that wasn't in Chapter Three?

Adventure Time: National Parks

abdocorelibrary.com/engineered-grand-canyon

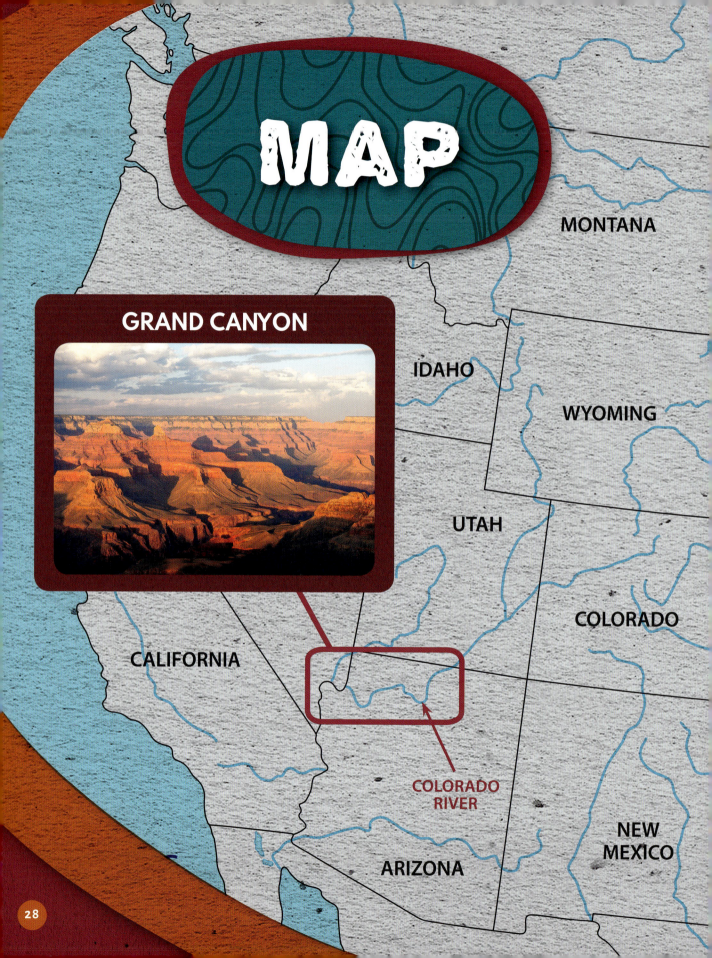

- The rock at the bottom of the Grand Canyon is nearly 2 billion years old.
- The canyon is 277 miles (446 km) long.
- The canyon is about 1 mile (1.6 km) deep.

Glossary

awe
a feeling of amazement and wonder

development
the act of building homes and other structures

eroding
wearing away by water, wind, and weather

minerals
materials from the ground that have never been alive

monument
something that honors a person or important place

rafting
traveling across water on a wide, floating structure

Online Resources

To learn more about the Grand Canyon, visit our free resource websites below.

Visit **abdocorelibrary.com** or scan this QR code for free Common Core resources for teachers and students, including vetted activities, multimedia, and booklinks, for deeper subject comprehension.

Visit **abdobooklinks.com** or scan this QR code for free additional online weblinks for further learning. These links are routinely monitored and updated to provide the most current information available.

Learn More

Chin, Jason. *Grand Canyon*. Roaring Brook, 2017.

Gagne, Tammy. *Exploring the American Southwest*. Abdo Publishing, 2018.

Index

age, 8, 12, 17
American Indians, 11, 21

Bryson, Bill, 13

Colorado River, 16, 18

erosion, 15–19, 27

Havasupai people, 21
Hopi people, 11, 21
Hualapai people, 21

layers, 5, 7–12, 15–17

minerals, 8

Navajo people, 21

Paiute people, 21

rivers, 6, 11, 15, 19
Roosevelt, Theodore, 22

size, 7, 22
Southern Paiute people, 11

Wilson, Woodrow, 22

About the Author

Martha London writes books for young readers full-time. When she isn't writing, you can find her hiking in the woods.